# THE ANALYST
# AND OTHER POEMS

by

Joseph Lawrence Dixon

Los Angeles

California

# DEDICATION

To Grace and Irene Dixon
Whose faith and understanding
inspired my poetry.

# TABLE OF CONTENTS

## OTHER POEMS

# THE ANALYST
*Preface*

The approach to this work is not entirely new, for it is neither possible nor desirable to escape entirely the traditions of the past. The fabulous characters created by the very real Spirit Land of Goethe and by the Presences whom Byron acknowledges in Childe Harold, as well as the airy personifications of Nature found in Shelley, are used in somewhat the same fashion here. However, to these entirely subjective denizens of the inner consciousness are added the obtrusions brought into the scene by modern thought. The conflict between the love so movingly described in the New Testament and the grim realities which we perceive, not only in the reeking jungles of the past but also in our present disjointed social structure where competition is partly concealed but is hardly less ruthless, forces us to recognize a group of new Spirits, hitherto unknown Presences, and strange aspects of Nature to which the classical poets were comparative strangers. If *The Analyst* has any new thoughts which would commend themselves to a modern lover of poetry, it must be in the musical utterance of things old and new blended together harmoniously as in the past. This is done here in deliberate contrast to the labored style affected by what are now called modern poets, who seemingly rely on the shock value of ugly and novel language to evoke the reader's interest, while they reject or deny what has always been regarded as the function of poetry; the depiction of the good, the beautiful and the true.

This better part of life I have attempted to describe as attacked and to some extent overshadowed by the negative influences which we cannot entirely escape, either in reading or in living; however, rather than to make the drama a real tragedy by having the gracious part of his existence utterly destroyed, it ends on a note of hope that the chief character, who has participated almost as a bystander in the struggle for the control of his mind, will at last conquer by his own innate sanity the obscure influences which tend to analyze and at last to disassemble his nature until he finally might come to feel that he has no reality, no life and no hope for the future. This state of mind is typified by the Phantom as a quasi-supernatural being, but Marne

3

realizes that what he has perceived as an objective presence is really a mere projection of his own thoughts — even though such thoughts are the powerful and dangerous ones which at last come to rule the lives of suicides and addicts.

# THE ANALYST

## SCENE I

*A Library*

(Marne seated at a table, reading. Enter Eleanor)

### ELEANOR

Good even, sir!

MARNE (looks up, surprised and pleased)

Eleanor! What —

(he goes forward and kisses her warmly)

'Tis late for you, now is it not?
I did not think your face to see.
Here, take this chair, and look at me!

(he seats himself on the table)

### ELEANOR

And are you all alone?

### MARNE

Oh, yes,
If I may count as nothingness
The creatures of my fancy's plays.
An airy fantasy always
Haunts my imagination's gaze.

5

## ELEANOR

And is that pleasant?

## MARNE

          Hardly so,
For I before their bidding go.
I am not master of my mind;
It drives before their fitful wind.
I cannot work, for lost in dreams,
The brightened future present seems.
So still I dream, and still at last
Dreams fade, unreal, and fleeting past,
The knowledge which I still pursue,
For which I seek, Life's pages through,
Eludes my grasp.

## ELEANOR

         O queerest man!
Can you the starry systems span
With human fingers?

## MARNE

         No, not I.
But should I therefore fail to try
Their measurement? Alone my eye
Cannot dim Neptune's disc descry.
And who has seen a number, say,
And who knows where a thought resides?
The march of Time we cannot stay,
Yet man the day and year divides.
He who is man is likewise fool,
Who tries to work without a tool.

## ELEANOR (continuing his tone)

Well, be it so, and your intent
Could find some yet mute instrument,
Which yet but sings of viewless things,
Which yet your fancy formless brings.
A glacier glitters in the sun
With clear and lucid depths, I ween,
But yet its peak, so hardly won,
Can only cast an idle sheen.
The Mother Nature you would know
Is cruel as the clasp of frost,
And in the lucid deeps below
Are bodies that have long been lost.
And is this, Rufus, not your dream?
What is there in its distant gleam
That it should lure you from the earth,
And the less errant ways of worth?
Look how I love you! Can you find,
With all the daring of your mind,
The calm security of faith,
That chases not its idle wraith?
In humble pleasures love can give,
And in the daily life you live,
You taste a pleasure unsurpassed
By visions shadowy and vast!

## MARNE

Yes, sweetheart, yes; your lucent eyes
Companion me to paradise!
I hardly know the ways of worth,
But you have drawn them to the earth.
Suffice it so; I yet below
Seek other worth we little know.
So human love and human hope
Shall not be frailly bound with rope —
The cordage of the wasted years
Shall not unravel to our tears.

7

Still, still we sleep; in youth must sleep
The knowledge age shall get and keep.
I will not sleep, I will not wait
For some still, certain human fate!
But, please you, let love's softest sleep
Companion me, so that I live,
While seeking what love cannot give.

### ELEANOR

Life?

### MARNE

In some sort. Life is many.

### ELEANOR

How you err!

### MARNE (quaintly)

Indeed, I have not any!
Through water, earth and empty air
I seek a life we do not wear.
And follow far, and follow fast,
No certain goal to reach at last.
But I have followed various paths,
And so, 'twixt Earth's and Heaven's wraths,
I shall be various to the end.
So that we two together wend —

(he bends his brow, and pursues his thought in silence)

### ELEANOR (rises quietly)

Well, let the matter rest. The end
Is various. If our fancies blend
Together, fortune wears no smile,

But let the clouds together wend,
And scattered blue is in the aisle!

(drawing on her gloves)

When Laurance comes, how will you sit and plot
The whole commingled plan; and I suppose
You can be hardly for a moment got
To muse on the moonflower and the rose,
Flowers of night and day. In your imagination,
Flowers are almost wasted, I presume?

MARNE (kissing her fingers)

No, I would clear the whole and vast relation
To give my fragrant flower standing room!

## SCENE II

CLOUDY DAY

*A Mountainside*

(Marne at the edge of a cliff, looking down)

## MARNE

Time was when I was gay and free. The time
Flowed onward like a happy, dancing rhyme.
The storm-cloud's nimbus and the thunder's roll
Kindled wild glories in my dreaming soul.
My spirit ruled the earth; I trod on air,
And knowledge beckoned up her winding stair.
My fancy was a harp: I swept the strings,
And awful music, hinting unknown things,
Rose at my fingers' touch. A half-formed song,
Sacred, mysterious, half-understood and strong,
With starry wisdom filled, flowed from my heart along!

But now
I bow!
I move before Fate's finger like a pawn,
A mad impatience drives me on and on.
Yet mid the elemental dance of all existence
My goal still lures me, all unmarred by distance.
Darkly cold,
Falls on my ear the maxim old:
"The harmony is long,
And short your song."
No matter how I race,
Time has the faster pace,
And the measured beat of his tireless feet
Will finally weary my pinions fleet.
Over the world, with resistless force,
Rushes a wind sublime,
Mighty and grand as the infinite source
Whence comes the march of time.
As with the passing of life I fly,
A picture of men I limn,
Driving like leaves through the autumn sky,
Blown by the wind of time.
Sink they at last, and their music sweet
Loses its silver chime;
Over their ruin, through wintry sleet,
Marches the giant, Time!
Ah, cold and bleak the prospect rises frore,
And vanished is the smile that Nature wore!
Her face shines dimly in the glass I hold,
Mocking with pallid glare my purpose bold.
Upon the snow-born images that pass,
The cloud-compelling force sifts down below,
And now the forms which blow across the glass
All come from winter and its peaks of snow.
Oft have I watched the airy forms that pass,
And blown their fleeting wraiths upon the glass,
But never life or living warmth between
Bloomed on the pictured forms, the phantom scene.
Above the hopes of idle years

I built a palace high,
And while it slept by silent meres
  The still, small hours went by;
Each flowery spring went pacing by,
  Till Fancy's palace vast
Crumbled with age before my eye,
  As I its ruin passed.
For love was human as the rose
  That blows beside the weir,
Whereby the lake-like water flows
  And murmurs all the year.
My heart was silent all the year,
  And weary was my eye,
Till once I stayed beside the weir,
  And saw my love go by.
Then all the thousand palaces
  I built above the storm
Were not like lily chalices
  That had adorned her form.
I let them be; I follow where
  I cannot move the storm;
I follow, follow all the year
  The shadow of her form!

(silently muses, he changes countenance)

Lo, as I spoke, the thousand palaces
Again in silence rose above the mere,
And voiceless rise the doubts and malices
That have my soul afflicted many a year.
The harp on which I erstwhile played
Echoes no longer to my song,
The music that my fingers made
Now rushes thought and will along.
A rider is my errant soul
Through shadows that around me rise,
My once sure path and chosen goal
Now deeply hidden from my eyes.
The reins are broken, and my steed

11

Leaps forward with increasing speed.
Nor would I stay my headlong course,
Though I ride off the very earth;
Farther than human is the source
Whence springs the tide of human worth.
Far in the misty distance rise
The fountains of the good and wise;
Their rivers, flowing through the world,
At last into the void are hurled.
And I haste on. The stream beside,
I on my unknown courser ride.
Before me roars, in plunge unslacked,
The thunder of the cataract!
My path leads into empty space:
Here shall I halt my reckless race?
No, from the Void a mystic singing,
Above the hollow thunders ringing,
Draws me still on. My spirit calling
Answers the rushing river's falling.
Forth into indistinct dominions
I venture on Thought's viewless pinions.

(enter Laurance)

## LAURANCE

Who is the friend with whom you hold converse?
Yourself? You might fare farther and do worse.
Myself, I cannot so; my barren fancies yield
No flowers, till social showers find my field.
    This you have ever lacked;
It is a singular fact,
Known to all peoples and climes,
    That only at times
    A thought or an act
On the wing of a beautiful fancy soars and climbs.
    Clouds of our own creating
    Shadow our sun alway!
Still for some fancied happiness waiting,

While we our lives away.
Hence, from beginning to end,
The fairest stars we could apprehend,
Through the realms of perpetual night
Wander, still lost to our sight.

(more gravely)

Two roads before each human creature lie:
One wanders on beneath the earthly sky,
Past green vales wending, or through gloomy gorge,
At last a chain from Earth to Heaven forge.
The other sweeps the labyrinth along,
Farther and dimmer growing to our sight;
Though we race on, with restless feet and strong,
We but explore the somber caves of night!

(with a gesture)

But let that all pass. My friend,
Since I have come to this place
I have hardly seen your face.
I confess that I hardly can comprehend
Why you have shown me so little grace.

MARNE (formally)

Indeed, I am sorry, but truly
You compliment me unduly.
You would be more pleased with a statue of wood
Than you would with me in my present mood.
How did you know I was here?

LAURANCE

Eleanor told me where.
She said you had left her house
And gone off in this direction,
As though you had been a mouse,

And she 'neath a cat's protection.
She said that your face was downcast slightly,
But that you spoke to her, oh, so politely!
    For very shame!
    Were I loved by her,
    Not wealth or fame
From her side could make me stir!

## MARNE

Do not reproach me; have you never,
Yourself, desired to be alone?
    Must be, forever,
I circle my heart with a wall of stone,
That manner kind, nor manner fierce,
The frowning battlements could pierce?
    Alone, the heart
    Expands to be a part,
    Infinite, alone,
    Nor bound by stony laws
    Which the Almighty Cause
    Has set on stone . . .
There are times when my mood is pleasant,
When I love the voice of my friends.
The future is lost in the present,
And all of its divers ends,
When Eleanor's image passes
Clearly before my sight,
Like the vision Hope's mirror glasses,
When we gaze therein at night.
And at times an unrest seizes fiercely my soul,
And drives it on, on, to an unchosen goal;
        Through unmeasured space
        I eagerly race,
For the veil seems to part, and the clouds backward roll.

But lo! my friend speaks of familiar things,
And slowly I furl my once far-spreading wings.
        I sink to the earth,

I laugh as in mirth,
But still in my voice a faint bitterness rings.

For the gigantic scenes which my fancy has shown
Are dark, and their kingdom is once more unknown.
        The vision is gone
        And the mist-veil is drawn;
And I walk on my way with my friend, alone!


### LAURANCE

Very fine! Of course you are not alone
When your lofty towers all of stone
Are brushed by the sweep of ghostly wings,
When your lofty towers all alone
Are touched by the sweep of viewless things!
            Is it not so?


### MARNE (vexed)

Half in doubt, and half in speculation
You muse on the disorders of creation.


### LAURANCE

    No, seriously,
Suppose we two together flee
To where the borders of all fancies blend,
Shall there I be your friend?
    No child or wife
Is found where borders of all fancies blend.
    Lo, thought, however rife
Is powerful, but all powerless wend
Your thoughts, save they are warmed by life and
love.

See, life beams from your brow, and from your gentle
smile,
        A radiance you wear not like a glove!

If that life dies, your features fade the while,
And death
Not always waits cessation of the breath.

Yet the life of earth is tame,
Ever and always the same!
The rose which blooms on the bush today,
How many thousands have bloomed before!
Still, the flower the last year wore
No more warmly reflected the sunny ray
Than that of today.

(gloomily)

And you as well,
You, who would study splendid Fancy's swell,
Must ever dwell
In a decaying prison
Which is your very clay.

MARNE

What spirit has arisen
Within your breast today?
Strange!

LAURANCE

What is strange?

MARNE (absently)

Strange contradictions which you voice pass and repass within
my imagination. Changeful your mind has become; a settled
change is fixed and unvarying within you.

LAURANCE (smiling)

Riddle-me-ree!

## MARNE

'Tis true, the life of man is not spent in those far places of thought. Yet far thought at times expands in every bosom. Tell me, what have you in mind, really?

## LAURANCE

I do but voice the thoughts that come and go;
   I have no settled plan, or fancy fixed,
But melted moves my blood, that age and snow
   Do half congeal to, in their fancy fixed.

## MARNE

I like not your tone entirely. It might lead to madness.

## LAURANCE

Mad? Is the lover mad at noon,
   With moonlight madness melted in his veins?
   Or is the old man mad, who at the moon
Gazes, and feels no fire within his veins?

## MARNE

Limitless thought has no pale or park,
   And passion has no bound,
But the bonds of sleep through that settled deep
   Create a void profound.
Many a mind lies where silence dark
   Reigns over all around,
And lost to music, can never hark
   To the all-creating sound!
     To that which lives,
     Life power gives
Over all moveless things.

LAURANCE (fiercely)

Still your mind clings
To the vision Hope brings!
There are many powers
Which rule over thine;
Many the hours
We to their will resign.
Nature thy mother,
And Time her idle brother
Still steal thy life away!
Over life's foam and smother
The tidal years hold sway.

MARNE

Nay, there is none
Greater, save One,
And that one ordains
A purpose to the years,
And but restrains,
To chide our foolish fears.

LAURANCE

And tears.

MARNE

For tears: —
For those who mourn, the coming years
Hold promise; blossoms watered by our tears
Shall bloom again, through little wasted years.

LAURANCE

I do not know.

## MARNE

Nor I. I only voice the thoughts that come and go,
Like you, and view their bright, their passing show.
    Myself, my tears are dry,
    And I look freshly to the coming time,
    And hold a purpose high.

    There was a time,
    So saith the poet's rhyme,
    When voiceless Time
    Brought forth a son who later conquered Time.
    My Mother Nature, see,
    Has brought forth me!

## LAURANCE

Complacent!

(seriously)

    But so you dally with the time
    Which while we talk, still steals your life away.
        What you have done today,
    You may not do when age has sapped your strength,
        And all your shining length
    Of days is but a spider's strength,
        Gossamer on the breeze!
        These mountains vast,
        And carpeted with trees
    Reflect the look eternal Nature wore
        A million years before.

## MARNE

    Yet lo! her ministers
    Move marshaled by the might of human hands,
    And Nature's fabric stands,
    Decaying, on Time's farthest strands.

Alone in the mid hours of the night
I muse what Nature has not consummated.

## LAURANCE

Nor God created.

## MARNE

Nor he created man
To be the voiceless creature of his will,
To float cloud-like through the eternal plan,
And brighten with his smile until
We cloud-like melt into that azure span.
   What man creates, is man's,
     But some destroy
   The far-created plans,
   And some enjoy
What others wrought, and bitterly cast down.
   Lo, Heaven's frown
Is on the dainty idlesse of the boy,
And on the scheming of old Avarice.
Left-handed thinkers tall,
Who vainly court fair virtue and fair vice,
   Shall perish all.

## LAURANCE

And vainly call
Their thoughts across the void abyss.

## MARNE (significantly)

Alone on heights of bliss
Sat miscreating mind of yore,
   And all the void abyss
He drank as the elixir of his life.

LAURANCE (stung)

Thy wife,
Or wife to be, is still a maiden pure,
And thou
Hast sat so long beside, that on thy brow
Is mild influence of her innocence.
Later, and not so pure,
You may a loss endure.

(with a dark smile)

I have a friend—I met him not long since,
And all the past and present he imprints
Upon the void imagination.

MARNE

Then past and present he must cure,
And all of the disorders of creation.

LAURANCE

This stranger is not such as you imagine.

MARNE

Say on.

LAURANCE

He is far older than my span of years,
And graver, too, although he wears
No graybeard fancy to the fire of youth!
But all the graceful melodies of youth,
And all the solemn mysteries of truth.
Or tales of simple innocence and ruth
Are mingled in my mind, as he has set them so!
For as the pulse of living, fast or slow,

21

Or languid steps that slowly come and go,
Or over dappled waters as we row,
Across my mind his fancies come and go.
Sometimes we walk and talk 'mid solemn pines,
In mountain dells where soft the sunlight shines,
And oft we move athwart the level lines
At sunset piercing through the forest's shade.

### MARNE

So Nature lies on couch your words have made,
With all her charms and blandishments displayed.
But will you make her innocent at last?
Proceed.

### LAURANCE

The age of innocence is past,
For the surveyor swings his alidade
Where once was the unbroken forest's shade.
Where now the mountain deer the streamlet quaffs,
Soon shall the mills of commerce grind and roar.

### MARNE

And do you mourn retreating footsteps vast,
Of presence who once graced the forest glade?
I have your friend found out. How fair,
How futile, are his liquid accents there!
Many the minds who magical the page
Of Nature made, and musical the mind,
Who with the graceful fantasies of age
Persuaded youth to follow and be blind.

### LAURANCE

And whence have you the knowledge that you need,
And whence the graceful accents as they plead?
Is then your wisdom like an autumn weed,

With feathery fronds for the next summer's seed?

### MARNE

Surrendered mind can faintly guess,
When weary of its idleness,
Which is the more, and which the less.

### LAURANCE
Surrendered? To what?
### MARNE
Solitude.
### LAURANCE
A voiceless entity, I fear.

### MARNE

Surrendered to the solitary mind.
You know too well what there is interlined.

### LAURANCE

And what is there you also know as well.
But if again its song would rise and swell
So sweetly, I would follow and be blind,
      But far behind,
My mind now lingers on the erudite,
Adding the sums that always come out right.
But talking with my friend, he o'er and o'er
Showed me the way to splendid Fancy's store.

### MARNE

What? Does your erudition enter that dark maze? And do you
dare?

## LAURANCE

Yes. Not that the middle mind is barred from happiness. But I would seek the mysterious pathways of even lawless Fancy, to find there the golden treasures Nature has hidden far from the trodden paths.

## MARNE

Where is the clue to take you there—and back?

## LAURANCE

Have you not watched a storm that comes at night,
And seen its mountains rising o'er the plain?
Among such dimness, majesty and might,
The mind might build its castles fair in Spain,
And find in them its lurking thoughts again
Made real and potent in those courts of Spain,
Where voiceless image of the artist still
Becomes colossus of the nation's will.
So, on some evening when the pendant moon
Adorns Night's bosom like a jeweled rune,
When clouds, slow-rolling from the formless deep,
Assume the spaces setting winds still sweep,
When the sun's beams, traversing heaven's arch,
Move as the clouds in solemn concert march,
And vaster castle the horizon sweeps
Than ever rose from mighty Fancy's deeps,
When lightning, like a many-petaled flower,
Blossoms one instant where the castles tower,
When life, all-pausing in its many sources,
Sees Storm, low-muttering, gather up his forces,
Then shall your spirit, mighty with the vast,
Across this void immensity be cast!

And every voice mysterious in that Void,
Of good or ill for social arts employed,
Created rise, never to be destroyed!

## MARNE

Strange spirit! Out of dim nothingness you have indeed called this vision. I mistrust it and you. Deeply, darkly, dangerously you dwell in rash schemes that would prove stark ruin were they consummated. It is true, I am attracted; my spirit answers, a rolling echo responsive to the lightning flash and play of your vivid words. But has your soul, slight wisp in the strong wind of your creative mind, measured its strength against things which have always effortlessly moved the generations on through youth and beauty, age and death? Slight soul of man, superior to the measured tread of time, can yet be whirled so far astray! In the blazing beauty of the sunny noon question these things, and you will see its light pale and sicken as the bright, beautiful world of the senses passes with your mind's eclipse!

## LAURANCE

You speak as one who knows. Have you already seen and walked at will through that world, the world of Fancy?

## MARNE

Not as clearly as you have pictured it. But often we prophetic speak of what we have only dimly seen in dreams.

## LAURANCE

And will you see my friend?

## MARNE

Not I.

## LAURANCE

What will you, then?

MARNE

I will abide on earth,
Pursue my life according to my birth,—

LAURANCE (bitingly)

And end your life according to your dearth!

MARNE

Let it suffice you. If the first succeeded,
So will the last, and little more is needed
To find the perfect, plain and simple ways of worth.

LAURANCE

You drag your words out in a dull montade,
Which Rhodomonte's wit would put to shade,
And I am petulant perhaps.
But look you now, is glory like a trade?
You will not, for one little-minded maid,
Forsake the field which Fancy's self arrayed?
Ah, birth and breeding, shaped to make you woo,
Now takes the tale, and nothing will ensue.

(with energy)

Where is the troth you pledged no mortal maid,
The daring force you conquered and displayed?
Alone you studied volumes for new light,
Alone you marked the starry courses bright,
And watched their changes through the hours of night.
Now will you read the mystic runes of night,
Or rest by fireside and by candlelight?
Oh, the sad tale! I sought it so, but still
I now must mourn your wax-like melting will.
When Eleanor has loved you, will it fill
Your mistress' eyes, to see you sitting still,

And mournfully obedient to her will?
Or will the winds, before the thunder's leap,
Waken your soul from out this vernal sleep?
Shall lightnings play and quiver in the deep,
And the departing breezes stilly keep
The voice of One who dwells afar, alone,
Never to answer to your voice's tone!

## MARNE

Truly I hear the thunder, rolling far,
But I am weary of that mighty war.
There is a soft, surrendered something, see!
Answers for all the world, and even me.
For once when Self gigantic loomed afar,
My mind and heart met in unequal war.
In momentary visions left the spot
This soul of mine, and ways of life forgot.
Look you, in turn! I seek to mend the place
I dwell in, and to halt for breathing space.
And would you urge me on, to travel far,
And spend my life in most unequal war?

## LAURANCE (turns away)

What beauteous visions filled this soul,
With lightning's flash and thunder's roll!
But now, distrait and tempest-tossed,
He thinks upon a moment's cost.
Pause you, my friend, a moment spend
In stilly reckoning the end!
The fiends that troop with horrid breath,
And gambol at the gates of death,
Are not, oh, no, so horrid quite
As plastered sanctimony's might.
And here's Old Age, with crawling flesh,
To grasp a moment of respite,
While devils desuetude unleash,
And try to set their matters right.

They'll let you blow the bubble bright,
And end it with a thunder-clap!
But you can set the matter right
After the bubble bursts, mayhap!
But let it pass, and have increase,
Like prophet-patriarchs of eld.
The granddames, nodding on in peace,
Will answer when their peas are shelled.
But concubine or little sign
Of love, you rock to sleep at night,
(Before the blazes basking bright!)
Will never set the matter right.
I bare no more; the bauble tore,
You never meant to wear in sight.

## MARNE

Pray you, have peace. There is no fiend as horrid as your breath, and the terrible words you unleash are as gray and grisly as old hags with broom and broth, and stinking with sulphurous ointment! Please you, at least tread cautiously this dizzy pathway you are so fain to follow, for life, let me remind you, is not like words, to flash out in wit and mimic grandeur, nor like gold, to be spent as the flux of sudden and most dangerous desires. Once lost, all's lost, for no one may retrace the shadowy pathways to the halls of death.

## LAURANCE

Nay, can you rest content, then let it bide! 'Tis true, the life of earth is passing dull. Not Wisdom but her spectre wanders there. Its sky is but a bowl of brass wherein are set two household lamps, the sun and the moon. Day after day, in dull, monotonous sequence, their burnished discs roll over the dreary plain. No whirlwind dances through the autumn leaves, no mellow sunlight glances from the stream! But yet, to live! why, that is worth it all. Better to be a snail in its shell than to run and fall like a gazelle. Better live for fifty years in honored peace and lucrative employment, than to blaze into view above the nations, and briefly move their lives to peace or war!

No! From your rusty scabbard draw your sword, unfold your wings, explore the caves of night! Where the foundations of the world are laid, there shall you find that hidden Key, or never, that shall unlock the door to those desires, that neither gold, earthly glory, love nor fear have ever quenched in the breast of man.

Arise! Arise! Hear you not far voices calling? Dull and faint, as from an immeasurable distance, the music of their singing rings upon ears deathless as their song . . . These mountains vanish before me, a heavy darkness encircles and weighs me down. Fearful and glorious faces alternately appear before me, and again withdraw into the mist.

The darkness disappears, and an indescribable glory shines, receding, faint to view. Over the vales and woods, past clouds and sunset air, gigantic visions float, where Titans appear and pass, with measured and soundless tread. And far, far beyond, into the Glory toward which all are speeding, the music marshaling immortal armies rings, rises and falls, passes on and on, till the very portals of Heaven echo again to the sweet sound of the singing!

(A cloud rolls up from the valley below, and the forms of Laurance and Marne are enveloped in mist.)

## SCENE III

DUSK

(Marne, walking alone down a gloomy by-path. He meets Eleanor)

## ELEANOR

Good evening, black bear!
(Marne shakes his head with a weary smile. Eleanor goes up to him, clasping a hand in hers and playing with it)
Now what is the matter with you today? Your brow is furrowed and discontented. Let me smooth it out. (She presses it with

her hand) Your lips are curved down bitterly. Turn them up—so! Aha!

(she breaks into a delighted laugh)

## MARNE

Oh, Eleanor! You are like a fountain in the dry desert of my life!

## ELEANOR

Fie on your dry desert! Were you not happy and good-tempered before you met me? So they say. And since, have you not been a sullen brute, morose, unsociable, short-spoken even with me? Truly I think this is the reason for your desert: you drain all your country to make my fountain—and not too much of a fountain either!

## MARNE

Sweetheart, there is a deeper reason: the scorching heat of summer has come, and the pleasant though turbulent vernal storms, that over the country swept, have vanished. Yet often in the dead of night I hear the muttering of distant thunder, and shudder to think with what a storm the drouth will break!

## ELEANOR

Why, what is it ails you? What is it should trouble you?

## MARNE (with face averted)

Would that I knew! Yet—do I not know, but fear to face the Thing— Hush! Question me no further! Leave me; I would be alone.

(Eleanor clasps him more firmly, and pulls him down to a seat beside her. Behind them stands a dim and formless figure, but neither perceive it.)

30

## ELEANOR

Leave you! Not in your trouble! When you have prospered say those words and poor Eleanor will wander off alone, to live or die. What is your worry? Let me know it. I will go with you, share every danger, all through the years of my life!

## MARNE (in anguish)

No—no—no! Of what avail is your death? You could but fail to endure the test — even if you could go where I must go! I too may fail. But though I perish in misery you cannot know the cause, nor save!

(Darkness)

## SCENE IV

### THE STORM

(Stormy. Enter Marne, Laurance and a Stranger, on the top of a cliff)

## MARNE

See, the sun sets, but still a soft light shines,
    And mantles the white bosom of the storm.
    Across its tracery and aspect warm
The rays are reaching in long, level lines.
But in the vale below the shadows lie
    Upon the roofs and homesteads spreading there.
    In the suspense, a sadness in the air
Steals to my heart, and all its tumults die.

## LAURANCE

But hark! to the huge, the awakening Giant,
    Ruling his forces on mountains of air!

Over the gulf hang his streamers defiant;
  Let us seek forms, that his glory may wear,
Look for the Beings, his mountains may bear,
Princes with power, princes of air!
Ruling the ruling ones, staying the setting suns,
  Only we dare!

## MARNE

Ah, but behind thee lieth the earth!
    Nursed thee at birth,
    Raised thee to worth!
  Leaving without a  sigh,
      Her sons go far and nigh,
      Seeking to leave their world,
        But at last are whirled
  Like autumn leaves to her bosom brown,
Lying as still at last, as they never had drifted down!

## LAURANCE

    Once together we saw
    Her womb and cruel maw;
    With dreadful appetite,
      Her children slight
  Devoured she, ere first the bright
    Pale beam of Heaven's law
  They, children of that Heaven saw!

(Laurance and Marne wander off along the edge of the cliff.
The Stranger looks after them.)

## STRANGER

There they go, proud mortals after the flesh! Their spirits sway
uncertain in each passing wind. The elder one is stronger, but
he too is weak, too weak to measure his strength against the
Immortals.

FAIR FORM (appearing beside him)

Must it go on?

STRANGER

It must.

FAIR FORM

Then misery to me. Tell it not in Gath, publish it not in the streets of Ascalon!

MARNE (looking back suddenly)

What is that, standing beside your friend?

LAURANCE

Do you not see? It is the wild plum tree, growing beside the little rivulet.

STRANGER

Would they know Wisdom to the uttermost extent of her resources? They shall. Would they overturn a stern but provident Fate, and themselves weave all the threads of their destiny? Yet even now the strands of Fate involve them and draw them on to this brilliant, rash and dangerous experiment. Come, ye powers and ministers of Destiny! Come!

(It grows brighter. The pale form is seen to be the wild plum tree. Three chariots rise from the gulf below, and hang poised by the edge. The Stranger beckons to Laurance and Marne.)

Here are the steeds which will carry you wherever it is your will to go. Spring to your places and away!

## LAURANCE

Open the ball! We follow.

## STRANGER

But think! ere you take this irrecoverable step! Not years of joy or mourning will blot out this night, and if its success be ill, not all the miseries you may afterwards endure will undo its consequences. So weigh the issues, nor lightly choose!

## LAURANCE

Choose! I have chosen since my earliest youth. Thought is a bitter herb, whose leaves I may no longer listless taste. Action is what I require. Come, to the movement; let us be gone!

## SCENE V

### COMMENT

(Through a rift in the clouds, dimmed to faint glory by the trailing mists, the cars of Laurance and Marne are seen. A shadow, as thrown by some unseen Form, lies black across the opening.)

## SHADOW

Make haste! Lean forward with eagerness, endeavor to hurry the speed of your onrushing coursers! Ere this night has spent her course, you will wish for a swifter power, with the speed of eagles at dawn, to bear you back to your old home on earth, which you can never reach again!

(another shadow moves beside the first)

## SECOND SHADOW

Why do you tarry here?

## FIRST SHADOW

To measure with my length the path of these. Look!

## SECOND SHADOW

It is only a small gain. One man—two men.

## FIRST SHADOW

No, brother, for they were noble as the morn.

## SECOND SHADOW

And like the morn shall end in night. But come! We shall see
them again, and to better advantage.

(breaks into song)

Come, come along, mountains along,
Rift through and cavern through, lightening strong,
Come, come along . . . . .

(they glide away, their voices dying in the hollow spaces)

## SCENE VI

### THE OUTER CIRCLES

(A platform and parapet among the clouds. Marne and
Laurance standing there alone.)

## MARNE

Have we not reached the peaks of Storm at last?

See that tremendous gulf lying open below us. Above us shines the blue sky of evening, now hidden, now revealed, as the upper-most reaches of cloud pile and tumble over one another.

Do you hear those voices? Strange sounds, such as stir the soul from sleep? Melting murmurs, ah, sweeter than the voices of the past? And look, the dreadful apparitions that steal beside us, and on, as if questing toward some unknown goal!

### LAURANCE

They are half-human. But their heads are veiled, and black audiences are dimly seen through the windows of their eyes.

### MARNE

Think you that they are in the flesh?

### LAURANCE

I do not know. Are we?

### MARNE

It seems that we have lost our guide. Would that he were here! Let us wait for him; here we are not harmed, and our human sub-stance seems to tread firmly the impalpable but crowding masses of cloud.

### LAURANCE

Not so! Let us on!

### MARNE

Rash!

### LAURANCE

Is this a moment to pause like frightened children? Have we

gone so far, and is it in your mind to stop? Let us quest on; naught can harm us, and if it can, what gain were it to adventure always through childish pastimes and play?

VOICE (like an echo)

With fair and childish phantoms, far away!

(startled, they look about)

MARNE

These horrible phantasms! See how they stream across the gulf. To what unknown regions are they flocking now?

VOICE (near at hand)

Look! Look! The Larvae, with Medusae —— (silence)

SONG

How they flutter, the Psyche-forms,
 Butterflies on the breeze,
Through the light, that beckons and warms
 O'er these ephemeral leas!
Come, let us on! Over this lawn
 Rushes the Phantom that flees,
Whom human mind follows, but blind—

VOICE (like thunder)

Peace, ye babblers! Come to me!

LAURANCE (seizing Marne by the arm)

Come, I say, let us go!

MARNE (shaking him off)

Can we tread the impalpable aether?

MISSHAPEN GOBLIN

Why not? 'Tis the IDEA buoys you up. He! He! (vanishes)

LAURANCE

Maybe the Inhabitants will tell us. (to a veiled figure who is passing) Stay a moment, friend! Whereto flee these spectres of the mind?

PHANTOM

Where you are going.

LAURANCE

No, we have lost our way and know not how to go or what path to take.

PHANTOM

Once you have come so far, you cannot miss it. However, a companion always lightens a journey. Shall we go together?

LAURANCE

Gladly.

PHANTOM

Cannot you cross on the airy breezes to the hall? I will make you a pathway.

(Raises his arms, swathed in robes like cerements. Clouds roll up to form a bridge, arched, and shot under by a beam of sunlight. They pass.)

# SCENE VII

## THE INNER CIRCLES

(A vast hall. Enter Phantom, followed by Laurance and Marne. The Phantom turns to them.)

## PHANTOM

Here in this hall the secrets lie,
Multitudinous ranged before the eye.
Matter and physical, spirit and force
Move on before you, in strangest divorce!
Say, ere you came here, could you the course
Reason of passion, feeling, remorse?

Now trace the strands that all glittering lie,
Weaving a tapestried life to the eye.
Secrets are sundered: back to their source
Track the first fluttering movement of life!
See the exhaustless, the ultimate force,
Move through the children, rise from the wife.

All things that are, all things that were,
Whir like vast wheels, and their cogs never err.
See the exhaustless, the undying strife,
Live in all forms, and in newer be rife;
New in the naval is war to the knife,
And booms in the gunshot, shrills from the fife.
Your mind which flees over these seas,
Seeking immortal grandeur and gloire,
Nestled with maiden who, lovely and shaden,
Was like a snowdrop pure on the hoar!
Now within these monstrous degrees
Would you seek, wanderer, doors without keys?

## MARNE

Have you no more, only that lore?

39

I too have measured, over and o'er.
Let me that door open, explore,
Now, to existent image of me!

## PHANTOM

But there are two: doors without key,
Doors which will open—which shall it be?

## MARNE

I, and of me.

## PHANTOM (carelessly)

What is't to thee?

## MARNE

In regions of the mind where thought may pierce
    Are many borders, nebulous and grand,
But with dark warfare all the aspects fierce
    Drive out fair, gentle Faith with iron hand.
Love is no love, that cannot even stand;
Faith is not faith, that goes not hand in hand.
So would I see myself as a fixed star
    Arise, and shine from an unceasing station;
Let burning thoughts, commingled as they are,
Appear as movements of the mind's creation.
Let Love and Hope their sceptres hold unmarred,
    And joy intransient reign o'er earth and ocean.
Such be the scene I view; the Soul unbarred,
    And the Mind's halls alive with bright emotion!

## PHANTOM

Earth-dweller, your spirit
    Sleeps in the dark;
Do you not fear it,

The heavenly spark?
As a flame you conceive it,
A beautiful essence,
Your fancy must weave it
According to thought.
Lacking its presence,
Your model is naught.
Before you a glass hung
Mirrors your being;
Around it a veil flung
Hinders your seeing.
And, in the mirror
Only the known
Wisdom and error
Ever are shown.
Break then the mirror,
Tear down the veil:—
Are you the nearer
The end of the tale?

## MARNE

Your words are spun out like a glittering thread,
But no meaning is hung thereon.
Your words are mere eidolons, brilliant but dead;
Come, or the night will be gone!

(The Phantom lifts his hands. An image of Marne forms in the
distance, seemingly gigantic, but far away. Thunder, which all
the while has been growling and muttering, now roars terribly.)

## PHANTOM

Hearken, O mortal!
Opens the portal
To immeasurable spaces!
Here is Thyself — behold,
O man of mortal mould!
Long, long

41

Hast thou, overbold,
Wandered afar from familiar places,
Where Being traces
Only the known, fair forms!
Heardest our song
Wandering lonely among the hills,
Sawest the storms
Rage, inextinguishable, over earth and ocean,
Heard, in the voice of love,
A whisper half-revealed,
Saw, with the velvet glove,
The sinews tense and steeled.
Through endless motion
Thou sawest faith, devotion,
Love, sacrifice, revealed,
But badest spring
Their likeness through such courses
As stained their heavenly wings.
There were the viewless things
Made manifest to thee;
Now their augmented forces
Again return in Me!
Now, nevermore
Thou mayest pore
Over the midnight lore with delight,
Or, in deep night
Rise past the light
Of stars set on eternal thrones.
Or, amid mourners' moans,
When Death sits on the smiling head
Whence life has fled,
Feel that still life,
Once in those fragments rife,
Risen to incorruptible glory, wears,
Through ceaseless years,
The fairest smile it bore
When Life's all-gracious moments passed before!
Where is Life's joyous dawn?
Gone, gone, gone!

Where has Love's presence gone?
On, on, on!
Ne'er shall it be
Pleasure to thee
To stroke that shining head,
Once Love is dead,
Once Life has fled.
Spirit of man,
That hopes and fears,
Knows not the span
Of endless years.
Each chrysalis warms,
And on the wing,
The Psyche-forms
Are fled with Spring,
And, having passed,
No more are glassed
Where once they sailed o'er liquid haunt!
As a romaunt,
Man's story, spoken, broken,
Fails like a mouldered token!
Bound by no bands,
His being stands,
Mosaic on the wall,
Where Fate has blown the colored sands,
A moment ere they fall.
No more may human dreams,
Which spun themselves to thee,
Rise from a heart whose streams
Were Eden-like to see!
Fold thy dark wings, O man!
Which hang now o'er the Void.
All that the mind may scan
Shall be for thee destroyed!
Thou hast sought to see
And be
That which is hid from all men, and thee.
But opened at last was the door
That leads to the black Unknown,

And standest at last before
The hanging veil, alone!
What now to see?
What now appears to thee?
A God? No!
Even as we are, so,
Dreadful, phantasmal Fates,
Surging passions and hates,
Sitting by million gates,
Rule over endlessly changing states!
Living? No!
Broken, battered,
Fragments once living, scattered,
Become in the darkness the ghostly Things
Wherefrom all being springs.

                              (with wild laughter)

See! See!
So will it ever be
With those who SEE!


(They stand, fixed by horror at the Being's words. Toward them moves the image of Marne, huge, vague as storm, moving at the beck of the Phantom's hand.)

Frail mortals after the flesh,
Caught in the fatal mesh
Of Circumstances, Law and Death!
Breath
Of the void and cold,
On these bold
And reckless explorers into the dim and old,
Come!
Here is the form you were wont to wear on earth,
Which birth
Clad with the spirit that elsewhere was never begun.
Sun
Shone on the glowing corpuscles and made them run,
Star
Beamed on the winnowing eyelids and let them sleep,
And deep

44

In the cosmos eddied the waves that, leap by leap,
Mounted, toppling, up to the height of Man.
Now scan
Thy nebulous vastness; be as the waves of thought,
And speed through the shining nerves to the central span,
And view, from the apex down to the pavement plan,
The height and the breadth of Man —

(through swirling mists)

Naught!

## SCENE VIII

### THE SABBAT

(The same. Enter Laurance, Marne and the Phantom)

#### PHANTOM (shouting)

How now? Where is your soul? Have you seen it?

#### MARNE

No! For you have not shown it!

#### PHANTOM

And if I showed it, would that atone it?

#### MARNE

No, for you, phantom that you are, can only show the dead shadow of a man's soul. But I defy your proffers and pretences.

#### PHANTOM (turning to Laurance)

And you? Does your faith stand firm also?

## LAURANCE (haltingly)

The force that drew me on to this strange quest
   Was founded on the things I saw and guessed.
Now like a cloud arising from the west,
   A shadow from without has filled my breast,
But still the old influence holds, and you
   Cannot withstand the earnest strength of Heaven,
   To which our strict attention shall be given —

## PHANTOM

— Till by the flaming, dreadful truth 'tis riven!

(He unwinds the mantle that heretofore has concealed the reality of his aspect. Before that death-like stare Laurance quails, and Marne half turns away.)

SONG (from out of the shadows and rifts
that lie around the hall)

As the meteor that trails through the starry sky,
         And vanishes,
As the flickering lightning that darts through the cloud,
         And disappearing,
Leaves but a roll of thunder in its wake,
         So are we.
But ever and ever again we return!
In the pale haze of even, night's glittering heaven,
         Our form is dimly outlined
We walk beside you and faithfully guide you,
         And follow you from behind.
When the firelog sparkles and the white snow darkles
         Through the window-pane at night,
While your dream of power expands like a flower
         And floats before your sight,
In your ear we murmur, and ever firmer
         Our fingers close on your heart;
We open your lashes on dust and ashes,

That your happiness may depart.
In the jungle we walk with the tiger,
On the ocean we roll with the waves,
But mostly we dwell in the breast of man,
Where the obscure depths
And the unknown caves,
And the vast, undiscovered spaces,
Like these cloudy hollows and shadowy hall,
Give us a hiding place!


(A bright flash of lightning, a loud roll of thunder. The forms of demons being to appear, dancing.)

DEMON (shouting loudly)

Where are they?

PIANISSIMO

Who can say?

DEMON

Here they are!
Their bright star,
Hurl it down!
Hurl them down
In the depths!
Where the whirling vapors
Extinguish their tapers.
Tear them to pieces,
Destroy them!
Take off your fleeces,
Ye wolves!
The music sounds louder, the dance increases,
Come here, my chosen, and dance with me!
(He seizes
Laurance and dances with him to the edge of the gulf, into which

they fall waveringly out of sight. The Phantom takes hold of Marne. There is a sharp struggle, and the Phantom is hurled away.)

### MARNE

Go back to the Hades from which you were raised, dark ghosts!

### PIANISSIMO

Ay, so we will, to your heart, which has become a Hades, and which shall henceforth be our home!

### MARNE

A restless home! You will find angels there!

### PIANISSIMO

So? We do not fear the angels, but the angels fear us.

### MARNE

I shall be there.

### PIANISSIMO

Alas, poor butterfly! You will soon beat the golden dust from off your wings.

### MARNE

Am I so weak? Are you so strong? Come, then, destroy me!

### PHANTOM

Fool, you are dead and are in Hell. Look upon my face!

(Marne, irresistibly drawn, falters before his awful gaze. With exultant yells the demons leap and gambol, advancing nearer and nearer.)

MARNE (recovering)

No, No! I yet am master, of myself and you. (with averted face) Oh, the dead eyes, that stare lustrelessly from their sockets, and spread their deadness throughout all my soul! It is not true, yet I am not true; it is a dreadful dream from which I cannot wake! Hideous monster, born of death and night, have you also dissolved my living flesh away from me?

(the dark shadows press nearer)

Away!

ALL (shouting)

No, *thou* away!

MARNE

I must. I cannot maintain my soul among you. See, I quit this hall and return to earth.

CHORUS (shrieking)

GO! We follow! We will be with you evermore!

ECHO (garbled and hollow, resounding from the walls)

Oh, Analyst! You have analyzed Yourself,
and the parts lie scattered o'er . . . . . . . .

RE-ECHO

Impossible to restore . . . . . . . .
To restore . . . . . . . .

49

# SCENE IX

(The library. Eleanor is discovered by the table.)

## ELEANOR

The house is so lonely!
No one is here, and I only
Stand in this room and wait.
Why, I wonder, is Rufus so late?
No one has seen him since yesterday.
Yet, that is not long for him to stay;
Often he has been gone longer.
But my disquiet only grows stronger.
Perhaps 'tis the thought of his look and words,
That hang o'er my head like swords
Since we parted the other day.
What did he say?
I could not understand,
But his words a strange fear fanned,
And as embers brighten at a breath,
So a dread like that of death
He has kindled in my breast.
"Dare I to face the Thing —
Dare I speak frankly, lest —"
What made his voice so ring,
As one in misery?
What does he see
At night when he walks alone?
Each day he has stranger grown.
What spectre is it can dwell,
What is it lies
Behind his eyes,
Those beautiful eyes, that I love so well?
If he would only come with me,
Then would he see
That Happiness dwells on the earth,

That music and laughter and mirth
Were created to gladden the heart,
That there is no art,
And no treasure-trove
Like the presence of those we love!

(In the deep silence that follows Marne enters unobserved,
attended by the spirits from the hall which have followed him,
and also by a group of brighter forms.)

### MARNE

Eleanor! Eleanor!
What are you doing here?

### ELEANOR

Why, sir, what do you fear?
Has my demeanor
Too forward grown?
Well, I confess,
I was alone,
And, you may guess,
Lonely as well.
What story, now, can you tell,
To account for your absence today?
Do it as best you may,
For your fault, sir, is very grave!
Have you lost all desire to see my face?
I once did not ask for what you gave!
Well, I forgive you with excellent grace,
Since you are here,
But do not do it again,
Or I shall fear
I have sowed my love like golden grain
On a bare and stony heart!

## MARNE

I will not do it again.

## PIANISSIMO

Never again
Shall in your heart be buried love's bright and golden grain!
Nor in that farther Spain,
Where Fancy's court has lain,
Castles shall move in grandeur before the heart and brain,
As cloudly move the seasons through sunshine and the rain!

## EROLOS (a spirit bright and dark by turns)

Never believe them!
In clouds and shadows leave them.
If Fancy seeks them, leave her.
What! Would you grieve her
Who was all the world to thee?

## PIANISSIMO

Shadows fall on the lea!
Soon you a shadow shall be!
Leave her!
You cannot ever retrieve her!

## EROLOS

Are your eyes so dim,
That darkness within you, extending without rim,
Blots out the brightly burning, beautiful world?

## PHANTOM

His eyes are dim.
Far is his being whirled!
Brought by the breath of one tremendous whim,

He is into instant and eternal darkness hurled!

(Marne has sat by the table, and listens to the voices of the spirits. Eleanor approaches and touches him with the tips of her fingers. He starts.)

### ELEANOR

What is the matter with you?
Why are you so sad and silent?
When you came I was glad,
For there is no joy for me
That equals the sight of your face.
But what is the harm if we never meet,
If we are lonely together?

### MARNE

Pardon, Eleanor!
It is not my fault.
Perhaps I shall nevermore
Gladden your heart again!

### ELEANOR

Art ill?

### MARNE

No,
But weary even of life's breath,
And my heart, beneath an unaccustomed weight of woe,
Labors, as on to death.

### ELEANOR

What has been done?

# MARNE

Naught has been done.
Between the set and rising of the sun
I have thought on—have seen how life begun
With formless monsters in the fluid deeps,
And watching where such life all formless sleeps,
Have traced it up to where my being keeps
Its state in grandeur, tithing all the heaps
Of bones and flesh that live on now in man!
And I have been brought to scan
More than immensities of form and void,
All without aim or plan or social good employed,
By naught enjoyed,
Only for one brief moment idly toyed
By Man, who rose to view what naught commands!
I too have seen the Beings without bands
Who, in the moments when Thought quiet stands,
Reveal the templed Truth, that without hands
Builded the world, and we that live therein.
Only that Truth I see,
But it is still to me
Formless and vague, indefinite and strange,
For Time still moves the shifting sands of Change;
Life, Death and Sin
And we that move therein
Are mutable; we range
Through the appointed circle of our lives,
But lightning rives
The heads of oaks: their crown of beauty shorn,
They are with others dying, old and worn
Blackness of night
Rises on all delight!
The pure, the good,
The fair, the strong and wooed
Are hushed at last in dark, eternal solitude!

ELEANOR (terrified)

Mercy of God! Can this be?

MARNE

It is. Look now at me!
    I stand,
But yet, on every hand,
One step may hurl me into instant death.

ELEANOR (whispering)

It cannot be!

MARNE

    It is, it is to me.
    I am not one to thee,
Who, on the yesterday,
Gave you in happy play
    Caresses!
Dresses thou worest then,
Thy sunny tresses,
Thy faultless face and mien,
Love's — presence — blesses!
Eleanor! Art to me
What I shall never see,
Save but in thee!

ELEANOR

But, if you love me,
What is there, can there be?

MARNE (sternly)

There shall be ever three
When we would walk alone.

55

When you would yield to me,
I shall have heart of stone.

ELEANOR (breathlessly)

Why?

MARNE

I am not I,
For thought and reason fly,
And burn in flaming circles whirling by.
Lives, that are transitory,
Compared to that far glory
End like an idle story.
They are begun
And ended, in few circles of the sun,
And my thought, whirling on,
Looks for myself, but gone
Is he who sped at dawn
Across the field and forest, and over the lighted lawn.
Dawn? Oh, God, at dawn!
Youth, too, has all withdrawn;
Its golden store,
Life's favors that you wore,
The form I came to love, your gracious presence bore,
Whose summer-lighted pleasance might flaming love
adore,
Vanish before the presence of coming winter frore.

ELEANOR

Then you do not love me more?

MARNE

I did love you, Eleanor!
Oh, my love! Love that is past!
All passes into universal gloom.

Lives, all in bloom,
Bewildered stride into the gates of doom!
Look at the beast, that rises, leaps,
Lies down to die, on heaps
Of dead, whose presence dread
Lie in the ground we tread,
Are broken with our bread.

(image of the Stranger rises)

### STRANGER

Dread
My presence which you fled!
Now words the phantoms said
Beckon the heart and head.
Swayed by the winds,
Blown by desires,
Your being ends
In fiercer fires!

### PHANTOM

Risen in vain,
This star shall stain
Heaven's own blue
Crimson of hue.

### EROLOS (dark)

Love shall be sweeter
As life is fleeter.
Rue is remembrance
Shorn of life's semblance.
Roses your being let gain,
Ere life shall wax and wane.

# ELEANOR

What is there come,
Suddenly dumb,
Over your voice and presence?
Let be the long, stern, gloomy thought,
Whereby this patient treachery is wrought.

## PHANTOM OF ELEANOR

I am not here.
I am not near.
My being clear
Is far away.
Where is my dear?
Why are you here?
Sadness and fear
Compass my day.
Have I lost thee?
Where, where is he
Who rose to be
More than the world to me.
No more I see
Beauty and grace in thee;
Sundered the way that we
    Trod
On our way to God,
By His decree!

(Larvae rise, thick, fast and furious)

## ONE

Laughter!
Thereafter,
Lips shall be dumb;
Drained of life's essence,
Lacking love's presence,
    Hither we come!

58

# PHYSIOLOGUS

We are as mannequins,
By page and page divided from the truth,
Who play, like harlequins,
With semblances uncouth.

### ANOTHER (hovering over Eleanor)

See, in her hair,
Festered, we lair;
Ghouls lie
Beneath the twinkling of a woman's eye.
Die, die
The first fair forms of life and love and youth!

### MARNE (breaking forth harshly)

I defy
These midnight reveries. The twinkling eye
You wear now, will be lovely by and by;
Yet now, forsooth,
I must deny
All love until the waking by and by.
Still nigh am I to ruth,
And youth and bloom and beauty. If I try,
I shall be succored by the gracious thought
Which you are, from this wilderness I wrought
Out of eternal Naught.
But now I go, attended day by day
By dreadful Thoughts, that bear me far away.
If ere my life is ended I can say,
"Love, be my life!" I pray you, pray you, stay!

### ELEANOR

Until what day?

## MARNE

Until, my life and tenderness returned,
I yearn for you as once my being yearned,
   Or till dim death
Hushes the fiend that stilly whispereth.

## ELEANOR

Has not my love already come to death?
So in my heart a still voice whispereth.
Now you are like a storm cloud, which the morn
Of light and love may nevermore adorn.

## MARNE

A storm cloud I have ever been, but one
That turned a brightened face on thee alone!
And from thy place arose the streamers slender
Which made that storm a fringe of trailing splendor.
Now in the night which has come over me,
How can I kindle light for thee?

## ELEANOR

If love were in the night, I still should find him,
And if I came, the darkness would not blind him.
But love nor light sits in your darkened presence,
And vanished is their summer time of pleasance.

## MARNE

If I have changed, the greater is my need,
The desolate, whom no one now will lead!
   Are you, indeed,
A butterfly which through a summer's leisure
Fluttered with yellow wings upon the breeze?
Who quits, when winter comes, the leafless trees,
The faded flowers, to follow warmth and pleasure?

## ELEANOR

I cannot find you — I have lost the way.

## MARNE

Then I must wend on, lonely, far away,
The bands of love you gave me yesterday
Dissolved and snapped. The barrier frail of life
May not endure until I find a wife
Such as you will not be. Farewell, nor find
One bright remembrance lingered in your mind
Of him, who was to life and beauty blind!

(Exit)

(Eleanor sinks down and hides her face in her hands, sobbing)

# OTHER POEMS

# INSPIRATION

Since he sketched with tools of stone,
Man has never been alone;
Shapes and sounds in various guise
Have descended from the skies:
Went with pilgrim's path of woe,
Ran through Volta's brain-pile slow;
Still far Inspiration's power
Instances each day and hour.

Will the modern pilgrim rise,
Searching through those very skies?
Yet in his dihedral lies,
Changed again, the strange disguise —
Diesel engine which he tries
Marred, not made, by his surmise.
Still through mind and being runs
Tissue of the shining ones.

# ROSE OF MY COMPANION

Rose of my companion, whither
Go thy sisters when they wither?
Do they gather by the river,
And in gardens bloom forever?

No, the rose in early blooming
Passes like the storm cloud glooming,
Like the flowers on the ling,
And all visitants of spring.

Other seasons, other roses;
Each in fitful trust reposes.
Snip! snip! snip! among the roses
Goes the Gardener, gath'ring posies.

Far away the All-Beginning,
Systems sifting, systems spinning.
Near at hand the systems sinning
Finish out each dreary inning.

In the silent, haunted alley,
How the wantons lurk and dally!
Surge on surge of bitter reasons
Held them back, through wasted seasons.

Who would argue and dispute
Betwixt none or bitter fruit?
'Twixt the silent, broken lute
And the heritage of brute?

Reason once, in giant wrath,
Pointed out no easy path,
Showed the winding paths of shame,
Rimmed and ribbed with spears of flame.

Fancy in an undertone
Wooed the crushed, the heart of stone,
Led me with her rosy art
To a garden far apart.

'Twas a visionary dream,
Where the things that are not, seem:
Could I walk no more alone,
Life would be an Avalon.

Nothing saved, and no one sinning,
As it was in the beginning,
Since the spheres with slower spinning
Set pellucid crystals twinning.

Reason had forbid that part,
So I smothered slow my heart.
Kingdoms which I had subdued
Faded into desuetude.

Then I bright Imagination
Set upon the regal station,
And a throne of greater splendor
Rose up from her duchy slender.

Wrinkled, wasted, hoary, old,
Reason follows Fancy bold;
Not an archer in her train
But outshines that ancient brain.

Now the song of bold dispute
Endeth, Faith and Reason mute.
Who would think it greater gain,
Got their godhood back again?

# AFTER THE LAST ADVENTURE

I tread the narrow byways
  Lying by meadows sweet,
As the last glows of sunset
  Soften day's fire and heat.
Life is a vast adventure,
  And all its ways I weet,
But when spent is the indenture,
  What shall its pathways meet?

I love the lowly village,
  With one narrow, winding street,
With its straying herds of cattle,
  And its picket fences neat.
I love the nearby valleys,
  And the mountains far away,
Whence the sparkling freshet sallies
  To dally with the day.

I see the fires of the sunset
  Fading from red to mauve,
And the scarlet thread to silver
  Glory is talking of.
Day, with its pomp and glory,
  Fades from the drifting clouds,
And leaves them faint and hoary
  As sages in their shrouds.

I leave the fires of daylight
  For the glowing lamps of night;
When Earth puts on her mourning,
  The city wakes to sight.
And the glitter o'er the temple
  Puts all fading dreams to flight;
Alike the wise and simple
  With shadows clothe the Right.

Far from the lovely valleys
    I tread the busy street,
And thread half-lighted alleys,
    With litter underfeet.
Pausing, I hear the quarrel,
    The scuffle and retreat,
And one lies on the pavement,
    Who will no morning greet.

I think the smiling valleys
    Are lying robed in shame,
When midnight silence tallies
    With reckoned deeds of flame,
Wherein one slight adventure
    Was blown like smoke away,
And vanished in the twilight
    To wait till Judgment-Day.

The Morn whose scorn shall stilly
    Crumple with fervent heat
The Earth all wrinkled-hilly,
    And hoary with long sleet.
Then shall no legal status
    With quo or quod complete
The writ mandamus issued
    For one last winding sheet.

The rocks shall blend with valleys,
    And elements effete,
When Life's last muster rallies
    Before the Judgment-Seat.
There shall no stated story
    With legends old compete,
Nor cynics old and hoary
    The words of Truth delete.

Like life, the lower trolleys
    Rush through the levels down,
From tissue-spangled follies
    In manacles of town.
But there is one adventure
    Which even town must meet,
That levels life and pleasure
    In one last winding sheet.

I know, some ancient stories
    Say life shall live again,
That Love shall spread his glories
    O'er the last haunts of men.
But meaning blends with censure,
    And vanished is the strain
Whose beautiful adventure
    Woke harmonies again.

I know, that lovely lilies
    Are swayed upon their stalks,
While the primroses palter
    Each wind that idly walks.
I know, that mighty galleons
    Are blow away in wrath,
That many lost battalions
    Tread the Serbonian path.

I tread the silence stilly,
    I learn the ways of men,
But withered is the lily
    That bloomed above my pen.
I hope, the haunted alleys
    Will keep my soul from shame,
While muted is the conscience
    That feared the force of flame.

Life's beautiful adventure
    I fear — it is so sweet!
And I deserve the censure
    Of sainted sages neat,
Who washed their hands with holy
    And beautiful desire,
While amaranth and moly
    Flower-crowned the chanting choir.

But I, with mission mended,
    Might deck in white attire
And touch the smoky torches
    That kindle household fire.
And the voluptuous valleys
    Might smile upon the hill,
Where witching Summer dallies,
    Foreboding good, not ill.

When the voluptuous pleasure
    Shall fade behind the rim
Of a world lost to sunset,
    And rid of every whim,
It may be my adventure
    Will but begin of late,
And after my indenture
    I wake to freedom's state.

# I LOVE MY SOUL

I love my own soul — love all of its coming and going,
Love all its flowers and weeds, and its seeds wide-bestrowing,
Its spacious demesnes, and the avenues fair of my growing,
And its wilderness leading to paths afar from all knowing.

Deep is my soul—as the boundless ocean is flowing.
Steep is my soul—where the far snowy currents are blowing.
But warm is my soul, as the summer its wealth in bestowing.

Far through the hills of my youth the winds of that summer are playing.
Far through the waste of my age may that sweet-scented season be straying.
But I love all the winds that arise—the mist that in distance is graying,
And the turbulent cyclone of fears, the branches of tenderness swaying.

Over my soul there rule many voiceless powers unseeing;
Firm in my heart there abide untold truths and their maxims agreeing,
Manifold precepts rude, odds and ends of old sayings,
Satraps rebellious to rule, causeless behests and obeyings.

There is no soft, sundered song there, that far apart sweetly is playing,
But war's red star, power of Mars, shines on the horoscope straying.
Evil my soul has known, swift and unthinking betraying,
With sullen remorse, like an unburied corse, all beneficent impulses staying.

But this I ever shall know: the end of my reaping and sowing
I shall love, be it blasted and black, or fair as the meadows in mowing.
For I love my soul; in life and youth, to the endless activities slowing,
In dawn, at noon, by morning light, and the sunset gloomy or glowing.

# APOLOGY

May be, my soul is not my soul alone,
But all things have contributed thereto.
May be, there is no mind that stands alone,
Fixed and constricted by its box of bone,
But through their garments, Words, our minds reach out
To Truth, which knows no bound, frequents no place.
May be, the brain, in bony carapace,
Has come down through the slow descent of time,
Impressed by the great seal of things that are
As much more able than ourselves, as we
Are potent, mobile, facile, more than crystals.

# THE PASSING OF CREATION

I walked the autumn forests, and I saw
On every branch, a host of yellow leaves.
The beetle burrowed in the rotting logs,
The butterflies sailed southward on the breeze.
The grape showed all his clusters to the sunlight,
And the few warblers left piped their sad lays.
I thought: the teeming life through eras varies
But little; in the plan they slowly change;
The snail is fitted to its convolutions,
The awns of grasses burrow in the fur
That carries them to new and fertile pastures.
All life is fitted for its living; also,
The species rise, that circumstances planish,
And the beast nears the god. What manner wears he,
The god, who fits into creation's plan?
The god has need of no created thing;
The semi-god helps only his great self,
And immolates the striving of the thistle,
The mild gazelle, the fire-eyed moth, the downy,
The furred, the scaly and the feathered creatures:
Useless the pictures of the fiery autumn,
Useless the burrowing of the tiny beetles,
For they shall perish by their kindred creature,
That now, or soon, shall need them not, usurping
For his own kind alone the naked spaces.
And shall the gods not do as mankind also,
Usurping for their kind the universe?
And shall not man, as an inferior god,
Be swept aside, as he would sweep creation?
And perish from the place that knew him once,
Since he is useless to the race that triumphs?
   O Man! Be thou not pitiless, or pity
Shall pass thee by, when menace unforeseen
Comes from the Future's catacombs, far vaster
Than any mind can dream of, nor can number
The habitants of dread, that may unmake us,
Even as we unmake the kinds of flowers

That please us not. If god thou be, be loving,
Be pitiful of all that lives and suffers,
Cherish the good, rather than expunge the evil,
And make a heaven of the universe.

# SONG OF NOLUTCE, THE HOUSELESS

(Who was an eye-witness: Saint-Saens only *heard* of the incident)

I linger in caverns, clammy, alone,
Lighted by candles of phosphor fire.
Alone in the charnel a dead man's bone
I seize, and rattle a melody dire.
Winds of the darkness around the stone
Swell o'er the horns of a hollow moan;
Coffin-drums sound in lieu of lyre,—
 Boom-a-la-boom! Boom-a-la-boom!
Hollow and horrid, arouses the tomb.

Twinkling the torchlight tempers the blast:
Faster and furious follows the cast;
Torrid theatrical troupe in the tomb,
Suite of the seatless, the dwellers in doom,
Dance to the tombless, the dwellers in gloom.
 Bittle-a-bit! Bittle-a-bit!
Castanets chatter, as wicked as wit.

Too-la-too-loo! Limpid, alone,
Clarion chanticleer calls to the morn.
Sin-sisters scatter, and under the stone
Slip the gray, gibbering ghosts at the horn.
Rattling tarsals that hammered the pave
Are smoothly upturned in the mould of the grave.
 Coodle-a-coo! Coodle-a-coo!
Sounds o'er the daylight and diamond dew.

# MADMAN'S SONG

A restless fever burns my bones!
  Burns my bones,
   Cruel stones!
To reach the fair blue sky!

This staring brightness hurts my eye!
  Hurts my eye
   Till I sigh
And weep and wail for quiet gloom!

In the darkness shines no bloom!
  Shines no bloom
   On my doom!
Let me wander through the flowers.

Through the sunshine steal the hours,
  Creep the hours,
   Evil powers!
Creeping on to age and death!

Youth and age shall spend their breath!
  Spending breath
   Wearieth,
So I sleep where Nature smiles,

But her space spends countless miles,
  Endless miles,
   Starry aisles!
Reaching not to Heaven's throne!

All the heart's sweet music's flown!
  Music flown
   Is the moan
Of a soul forever lone!

# PIANO

Little clouds at play
Burst and paled, one windy day;
Pallor pent
In the rent
Grew to steady rain and gray.
In their little windy way
Piled and tumbled clouds at play.
Grumbling thunder, rolling round,
Sounded under, underground,
Till a hollow roar profound
Made profundo harmony.
Savage skill
Sounded still:—
Swelling stilly underground
Ran the melody profound,
Till the gnomes and elves, embrowned
By long toil, caught the sound,
And with anvils clinking clear
Forged an instrument profound;
Technique, skill and technic skill
Molded, twisted to their will,
And their anvils clinking still
Sounded in the treble notes:—
All the clear and golden motes
Huntsman moted merrily,
And the brook past bubble boats
Sounded, floated, verily.

Bitter battle in the notes
Often marred the huntsman's motes;
Westward wafting wind and wave
Through the echo murmur gave,
Wildly weeping, windy will,
Westward wailing, wandered still,
Turning in a treble trill,
Wailing whisper wandered shrill.
Further form of flute and fife
Wildly waxed o'er subtle strife,
Over harmony profound,
Sounding low and underground.

Rose in ruin all around
Muted music underground,
Melted murmur in the mist:—
Faded, and the fancies list
To the murmuring no more.

# AN IDLE PICTURE OF THE MIND

Night withdrawn
Sat upon
Morning-crested mountain cleft.
On the lawn
Lay a fawn
That the fallow deer had left.
Limpid valleys lay below;
Higher gleamed the peaks of snow,
And one might a handful throw
On the gorges far below.
In the fuller light of dawn,
Little leaguer of the lawn
Lay, and long the light thereon
Gave reflections far and near,
For the ice was crystal-clear,
And the grasses grew as near.
Lined with grasses lush and cool,
Sparkled icy little pool.
Limpid light lay lost beside
Crystal swelling of the tide,
Where the fish and minnows hide.
In and out the stony side
Finny whiskers slowly glide.

# A TALE OF BORNEO

Beautiful blow
Breezes slow
Over the island of Borneo.
Negress slow,
Humming low,
Paced the tropics of Borneo.
Beautiful breeze
Out of the seas
Blew o'er the lowlands and lagoons low.
Sweet and slow,
Breezes blow
Over the isle of Borneo.

The rounded form and the pouting lip,
Some one observed from the stately ship.
Beautiful blow
Breezes low,
Over the lagoons so long and low!

The stately ship
Swung in the dip
And roll of the seas on that trading trip:
Man and wife,
In termagant strife,
Startled each other with wordy war.

Love fled afar,
The wordy war
Took form and substance of settled strife,
And waves that sip
At the lagoon's lip
Something bore o'er the harbor bar.

The wordy strife
Took form and life,
And muted something from vast afar,
That called again from the harbor bar.

Beautiful breeze
Spread o'er the leas
Rippling wavelets of tender grass,
Till in the glass
Of the lagoon's mass
Melted the form of the southern star.

On the mirror glass
Took form and mass
A ship's boat oared by a German churl,
And the paddle's dip,
Like a pouting lip,
Broke the smooth outline with graceful curl.

So the slow, good girl
And the German churl
Parted afar as their natures are.

# THE PORTRAIT

At the hour of vanished daylight the pigment partly dried;
The artist opened his window and gazed at the countryside.
All day, as had fiend possessed him, he had daubed and patched and tried,
And from that mass of color now a living beauty lied.

He took of the tinsel stucco and portioned it out with care,
And marveled over the magic tint that lay in the lady's hair,
The gauzy wings of dragon-flies that circled her shoulders bare,
And the waste wisteria woodland, that canopied beauty there.

The artist opened his window and gazed at the sunset glare,
Where the molded clouds, like figures, passed and repassed—so fair!
Till the fleecy white of angels caught the tints no angels wear,
And the shapes of stooping devils dropped down on the winding stair.

Then lays of lawless Borneo sang in his lurking mind,
And the lady laughed, whose looping locks over her shoulders twined,
And with kisses red as the clouds o'erhead the picture he had lined
Lured him along, while a silver song tinkled upon the wind.

Out in the dewy starlight, scent of a woman's hair;
Borneo beauties passed, repassed, close by the woodland weir,
Beautiful figures danced and looped clouds in the sunset air,
Under the lodestone star of love, glowing and burning there!

Beautiful godlike heroes slew dragons of sea and air,
Beautiful asking maidens lay, trapped in their own despair.
Breeze that was blowing along the lea lighted upon the pair,
Wooing and doing by silver streams, under a winding stair!

Out of the distance a Figure drew; his form shut out the cloud,
And moved the mighty mass along, that groaned and rumbled loud.
He laid his hands on the painted scenes and whispered, awful-browed,
"Be all the mind and reason flown, wherewith I thee endowed!"

And like a tinsel paper screen the painted pictures torn
Crumpled and fell the worlds between, revealing mountains worn,
The seas and valleys heaved aloft, the sills of earth upborne,
And lastly, lighting on the lawn, the level, liquid morn.

I slept beside a little mere,
An early wanderer through the year:
I woke, I walked; the crystal mere
Gave look for look to eager seer.
Now looked the limning fancies there,
And made no movement o'er the weir.

Beside the plash of waterfall
I built at ease a cabin small.
The bower of trees I intertwined
With lacy flowers, and I lined
The rough oak logs with earthy clay,
To stop the north wind's angry play:
I built a cottage by the fall
And interlined the open wall,
I took the bracken and the furze
That every wind in movement stirs,
And made them fend the winter's might,
And still contain the warmth and light.
Nor mine, I wist, a foolish life,
Pursuing movement, words and strife;
No slighting look nor idle quip
Gave answer to a pouting lip;
In fall I heard the water drip,
In spring I watched the bumble sip.
Life, life at ease among the trees,
Mid Nature's song of slow degrees,
The quiring slow of melodies
That rose and died among the trees.

Now whilom in an idle strain
I fell to thinking I would fain
Have mistress of the heart and brain,
And striving on, some end attain.
I thought of blooming gardens there,
And city-towns beyond compare;
I thought of stately pillars bare,

And buildings towered in the air,
But paused awhile to note, connote,
And note again, the linnet's throat,
Joy-pealing spring into the air—
That mingled with the sunlight's flare,
A living flame, then, all dismayed,
Retired within the mantling shade.
I thought of gods, who with the brute
Now lie in stillness underfoot,
Mouldering down into the sod,
That owned nor animal nor god.
I heard the quiring murmur lisp,
All-ending in a twitter crisp,
Where bird that swayed on grassy blade
Peered up at me, all unafraid.
Within the gloomy brains of men
I noticed many a twitter then,
Within the animal I saw
The acting of a moral law,
And in the god, far underfoot,
The actions of a sullen brute.

Pensive, and prisoned by the trees,
I took the song of slow degrees,
The quiring that through centuries
Sings over what the poet sees;
The animate and lordly brute
Shared in it, though his voice was mute,
And many the shallow brain of man
Rollicked upon its timbrel pan.
But oft the slow, the ancient plan
Looped up the mere thematic span,
And in the drama of a word
Spoke the slow opera unheard.
With teeming trills and sudden scale
Was woven the harmonic veil
That wrapped the Figure hushed and mute,
Who caused these murmurs underfoot.

The gods descending from their span
Lapped with the brute again in man,
And many a harsh and brutal law
Filled savagely his hungry maw.
The silken scarf and plaited straw
Clothed eagle beak and eager claw.
But with the rising of the brute
Rose maiden answers like a lute;
Like mute and unprotesting doves
They fell before the eagle-loves,
Who bound them with an iron chain
Of fierce desire, and fled again.
Nor love maternal in its force
Could eagle from the dove divorce,
But in the slow, the seasons' chain,
They grew into a feral twain,
Where good and ill strove hard until
They nested on a craggy hill.
There, unexposed to Heaven's stroke,
Which rends the vine and tears the oak,
They ruling rest, and ruling fly,
And rear their race beneath the sky,
A scourge of earth, and make its span
Communal—to the mightiest man.

A decent scourge, like slow disease
Fell over hearts beneath the trees;
The murmuring rivulet withal
Went brawling past the home and hall;
The bower by the waterside
Love's softest play was wont to hide,
But then the twain of decent strain
Suffered in unrestricted pain.
The parents slow and soft of speech
Met insolence and sonship's breach,
For in the rising of that tide
Was season's brutishness denied.
Though sanctified by innocence,
They frowned on pretty love-pretence.

In grinding of the moral law,
All sifted out but husk and straw:
Now the old pair rehearsed in vain
The stony laws they graved too plain.
For man has part with animals,
And pours hot blood through their canals,
And through its guiding heat and zest,
Love's sweetest visions stand confessed.
What though the brain, grown cold and clear,
Holds nothing near and earthly dear?
Better the presence of the brute,
And warm affection leashed and mute.

So on I moved my mingled measure,
And sifted out bright poet's treasure.
The mere reflecting forms of dreams
Were broken oft by errant gleams.
The babbling stream half learned the spell,
But broke it with a plashing swell.
Then I the magic old resigned,
And set myself a road to find,
For where the movements of the mind
Stir, there are rifts concealed and blind;
There start the turtle and the hind,
And there the monster has reclined.
The horrid demons of the pit
Upon the trees like roostlings sit,
And gaze with unawakened eyes
On bestial orgies they despise.
There are the dragons whose fierce breath
Poisons the tissues, worse than death,
A lifelong agony endured,
And only in the crypt immured.

There are the angels fair as dreams,
The pair new-waked by Eden's streams;
There rise the blisses of the world,
Through Heaven's portals dewy-pearled.
There, deep in hearts where concord speaks,

Man's noblest yearning beats and seeks,
Over and o'er again the sage
Garments the truth, and glowing Mage,
There shows what he who knows must oft
Miss with his mighty sweep aloft:
So artist and the wise arise,
And build man's palace in the skies.

But it is well from magic dreams
To turn, and watch the flowing streams,
The furrow turning from the plow,
And all that binds the here and now.
For in the thoughts' faint, distant seat,
One loses taste for bread and meat,
Nor comes to feel the vital heat
Flow through his veins, in home or street.
Look on the world with passing eyes,
It may be, but no soul despise.
So never shall the demons throng
Around a soul devote to wrong.

# A BED-TIME STORY

## *Preface*

Hush, my children; you shall hear
Words that fill you full of fear:
How the multimillion kind
Battles on, in tumult blind,
How the unicellular
Steals upon the mind at war,
How you are the axled car
That bears what an avatar!

## *The Tale*

Once there was a birdie blind
Singing in a silent wood,
Singing from a vocal mind
To a silent multitude.
But the pangs of hunger crude
Mastered numbers that he wooed,
So the lovely interlude
Ceased in toil for daily food.

Ages passed: a bird we see
Who has shortened up his wings,
So he left the air to be
With the arboreal things.
But his voice was lost in sleep,
And he settled through that deep
Till his arboreal leap
Grew a slow and cautious creep.

But his instincts rose in dreams,
As upon the ground he lay,
And again he swam the streams
In a dim, aquatic way.
Once again he pierced that deep,
High and clear above all sleep,
And his spirit's lofty leap
Mocked the ground where he must creep.

### Resume

What the ages not immure
Is the stream of life-blood pure,
Poured and drained, in changing measure,
At the idle hest of pleasure.
What the sages through the ages
Miss, is not the easy stages,
But the sudden rise of mind
In a creature blent and blind.

# METEMPSYCHOSIS

They say that Eros is the eldest god,
    And this I know:
I knew you ere each rising pod
    Its pollen threw below.

Or ever the hills were built,
Or raised themselves like a mother's breast,
    We in the Laurentian silt
        Together were pressed.

Our kiss was the mutual touch
    Of Medusa's trembling streamers,
And in them was latent as much
    As now moves enamored dreamers.

Things without knowledge, unknown to story,
    First broke through inviolate chastity,
And the eremite nucleus migratory
    Became, in conjugate ecstasy.

# DIM DIALOGUE

## ASMODEUS

I viewed but the fortune that followed us home,
I sat in the silence that settles around,
When windless fell spirits arise from the ground,
And gibber, and cower, and gather near home.
I live in your heart, but I have no more place
Than I gibber, and cower, and settle in gloom.
You live in my fury; I live but a space,
But you see in my presence a foretaste of doom.

Whither the wind of the earthly love
Blows, I follow the bleeding dove.
Willow on willow I heap on the pair,
Willow on willow they guiltily wear.
They are scorned by the blest, and they snatch their repose
Beneath the long shadow that gloomily grows.
Let us list at their tent, for their voices are blent
In a song of such lives as in pleasure are spent.

# PLAINT OF THE LOVERS

We wore not the willow that rests on our arms
While youth's smiling graces enlightened our charms:
     Our curls were yet sunny,
     And sweeter than honey
We tasted the honey-wine deep in the heart.
But wore we the willow when fell from our arms
The roses of summer, the faster we fled;
Not alone from the roses of youth must we part,
But flows no more honey-wine deep in the heart.
We wasted the summer, the summer is fled,
And hoar is the silver that covers each head.
     Cicada! Cicadee! Chirra! and chirree!
Do you think that the moonlight is fading for me?
     (pianissimo)
     Cicada! Cicadee! Chirrup! and chirree!
Oh, the sight in the distance is painful to see!

# THE ARTIST'S DREAM

(Artist, alone. The study is half darkened, but the pencilled flames from the hearth leap and throw dancing shadows on a marble statue, *en pedestal.* By degrees the dancing flames subside and the soft white stone grows in the shadow more alluring, sweetly sensuous, and all at once it moves with dancing steps over to the window seat. Lopsides, a material shadow, detaches himself from a dark corner and follows her with the awkward movements of a satyr.)

## LOPSIDES (smirking)

Began the ball. What follows?

## SONG (plaintive)

When spirits follow, fancy-free,
　　The irksome fellow is delightsome,
Delighted but to see and be
　　Released from darkness long and frightsome.

The lissome latitude is play,
　　But just to be, is service penal —

(Other shadows gather, talking at random in harsh tones until unintelligible gibberish results, and only the next rhymes, "lay" and "venal" are heard. A croaking caucus then takes place, gradually predominating over fluty murmurs subduing into whispers. A tall gibbon-like fellow steps forward singing "I am from Mindanao," but is instantly suppressed.

The artist starts up with an abrupt gesture of dismissal. The intruders vanish, croaking, except one fair spirit.)

## SPIRIT

I am the painting spirit.

## ARTIST

Good. Then paint this. (Reads) "The wind from NW was blowing over the hill ten miles distant. A lot of clouds blew over, hiding the stars except in places. It blew through some trees standing by a meadow and made a faint sound. The stars were of but small value, and gave less pleasure than the darkness did discomfort."

## LOPSIDES (who has returned)

A trivial incident, I am sure!

(The spirit flickers to a final flame. The artist rushes forward, entreating.)

## ARTIST

I pray you, stay, and give my defects voice!

(But the figure vanishes, to be replaced by another.)

## TUTRA (a small, still spirit)

Look you, do not use such trivial words, or the meaning will be even as they. *Wind* has too strong a cast, and the subsequents which naturally belong to it would not suit the complexion of your narrative.

## ARTIST (chapfallen)

I cannot follow such a tenuous thread of explanation.

## TUTRA (unheeding)

Let us say *breeze*. The northwest is a region of ice.

ARTIST (indifferently)

A cold breeze blew from the Northwest.

TUTRA

Better, but wanting much. The breeze was not cold, but from a cold region. Moreover, *cold* does not companion well with *breeze,* as *wind* does not. Try a trope, too, to vary the monotony of *blew.*

ARTIST

A breeze rushed down from the frigid Northwest.

TUTRA

Copyist! But persuade it to a metrical murmur and let it stand.

ARTIST (interrupting)

Why metrical? Has prose no value?

TUTRA

Oh, yes, in prosy subjects, large as life! Much prose, so-called, is metre not constrained, but flexible. But the measurer should be as careful of his feet as if literary criticism would scan and cavil!

ARTIST

Breezes swept down from the frigid Northwest,
Over a hill many miles away —

TUTRA

Oh, your trochees and anapests! Pause and stipple the colors on the second line, would you lure the painting spirit back to finish form. Let the first stand alone — full stop. Now, it is manifestly impossible to — oh, here she is again!

(suddenly the finishing spirit returns and sings:)

Breezes sweep down from the icy Northwest.
Midnight-black
Wrack
Of wild, writhing clouds, pressed
And scattered and folded and battered and molded
By the roaring wind pouring and far away soaring
Over the world's high crest!
And the stars, through the molded bars,
Shine from the caverns of Night!
Spangled and glimmering,
Spreading far-shimmering
Tangled blazes of light!
But the breeze through the trees that guard flowery leas
Moans in low tones and then far away flees
Over the liquid seas!
At night
Shines dim light
From the heavens star-bright,
But there flies through the skies the same cloudy disguise
That Nature has worn since her children were born,
And her flowers, wind-torn,
Mourning wait for the morn.

(The study darkens completely, and the dreamer's mind is veiled in sleep.)

# BOATING WEATHER

Breathe and blow,
Lightly go
Breezes born of the boating weather!
Over the white-capped waves together
Dance all the darling boats.
Over my view passed a plume and feather,
Passed, as sails o'er the boating weather
Pass where the barge-buoy floats,
Passed, as the clouds that silently drew
Out of the morning-deserted east.
Over the west and its beautiful blue
Their shadow came, and blackened, but ceased.
For east is east, and morn is morn,
But the westing sun is not all forlorn.
So let the plume and the feather pass,
As passes the beauty within the glass,
To flush the lips as they eagerly drink.
Wine-red passion upon the brink
Trembles, though glasses are crystal-clear,
But sediment settles, and lips shall shrink
From the sullied glass that was crystal-clear.
The morning over,
Passes my lover,
As he passed from my heart and mind one time!
Not all the power of words and rhyme
Can ever recall that olden time
When his presence dear
Was crystal-clear,
And morning sails under cloudless weather
Danced o'er the beautiful blue together.

# MY LADY

Once a lady, dark and rare,
Braided roses in her hair.
Seated on that ebon throne,
How their beauty on me shone!
So I spoke, with words that clung,
Slowly faltering, to my tongue:
"Give me roses that you wore!
I will love them evermore."

But a lady, tall and fair,
Wove white lilies in her hair,
And the winds of passion, blown
Through the roses, all had flown.
But my heart was warm and young,
And unceasing music sung:
"Give me lilies that you bore!
I will love them evermore."

Came a lady, debonair,
With no flowers in her hair,
But her face like flowers bloomed,
Till the roses darkly gloomed.
Never lilies were so pure,
Nor their grace will so endure.
Not her flowers I adore,
But herself forevermore!

# VIOLETS ARE NOT FAIR

Sifting song
Sounded strong
Over little parted ways;
Sun was dimmed by mellow haze,
Glory-gilding day of days.
To the senses, mild and clear,
Came the linnet's warbling note:
Out of liquid sounding throat
Pouring music far and near.
In the daylight, sounding, clear,
Through the ways I led my dear,
By the land-locked salmon weir,
Where the dewdrop's diamond tear
Gemmed the grasses. To the ear,
Sounding o'er the silent mere,
Boggy bittern boomed. Anear,
Spotted snake in silent sloth
Lay upon the velvet cloth
Of the lawn.
Sat thereon
Dully, light that from the rill
Sparkled in resplendent shine,
And I gazed thereon until
Hand of sweetheart stole in mine.
"What assails you, dear?" she said.
But I only hung my head.
Spotted snake of leaden hue
Lay in clumps of massy blue,
And the little tears of dew
Stirred, and trickled from the grass.
Only saw a looking glass
In the violet-mantled grass.
Dreams may come, and dreams may pass,
But upon the velvet grass
Only saw my darling sin
Sitting still and couched therein.

# PROGRESS

Alone upon the shores of farther thought
I tread, far from the murmur of the crowd;
No footprints mark the strand whose ocean, Truth,
Is as Phoenician sailors found the sea.
How now the nations of the world would rise,
As once they rose to maritime renown,
If they could venture from the time-fixed thought,
And sail at will Imagination's main!
We, who are creatures of our own produce,
Cannot maintain our former savage state:
We are as vanguards of an armied train,
Which moves us on, with slow, resistless march.
No more we lie in devolution rude,
Whose barbaric endowments ruled the past,
No more the nodding centuries may bring
A bright renaissance to yet nobler thought.
With Time's last sands we play, while trooping past
Go remnants of our former modes of life:
Times when we grappled with a savage foe,
Or fled like deer adown a mountain glade;
That which we followed in dead earnestness
Has now the studied semblance of a game.
Now without echo come the foemen dim,
Who never threatened in man's savage state,
Nor now the remnants of the animal
Can fend away the danger to our state.
Brains, and the merger of huge capital,
Produce from laboring masses mighty works,
But who directs these ancillary tasks,
Making them serve the progress of the race?
Not men, for many masters drive them on,
And lead in chains the few who would be free.
No modern heroes seek the golden fleece,
Boldly adventuring on new seas of truth.

At most they linger in the antechambers
Of princes absent from their own dominions,
Meeting the scorn of idle clerks and lackeys,
Who hold the reins of power in listless hands.
No longer saints and heroes fire the mind,
To add new glory to man's ancient race,
But gloomy Self and Discord rule the age,
And Truth's pale taper sinks and vanishes.

# LOST ART

There was a human soul
Who, in his solitudes,
Listened to quiring voices
Of his native plains and woods.
His nights were the harmonies,
    Ineffable, alone,
That, in the sculptured mountains,
Engraved their lines in stone.
His haunts were the crystal fountains
And the pellucid pools,
Where the heavens gave clear negation
To the evil books of rules.

*Evil is the hortation*
*Spoken in heat and spite:*
*Nature gives clear negation*
*To the evil men may write.*

But the soul, caught by learning,
Leaned on the desk it found,
And to the world returning,
Let its ties twine around.

The solitudes, spirit-haunted,
Enfolded him not again,
But each morning he was daunted
By endless processions of men.

    Men, men, men — endless processions of them:
  They dived in the pools, they ascended the heights,
    Swarmed on the frozen deeps,
Till the microscopic dimensions of the soul that remained unto him,
    Even amid the rubbish and refuse heaps,
    Could not hide from their numerous lights.

Lights!

Not light, but the numberless lights,
That stared, with their pin-point eyes,
That glared, with their merciless mights
On the soul microscopic in size.

And a line of unending tomorrows
To no quietude returned,
For cyclic change, like an angel's sword,
Over that gateway burned.

Eden he could not return to, so to the cursed ground
He betook him to delve, and planted the vine and the fig,
But the wild herb often withered, as the fruit was astringent to taste,
And the sweat of his face could not soften the arid ground he must dig.

Then from the Scriptural curse he broke loose, and journeyed afar,
And as a disguise he put on a resemblance to men,
And drove with their multitudes back to the habitudes old,
To find in their beauty surcease from his sorrow again.

But men's footsteps and pavements had entered the glens and the mountains,
And the highways unending a pattern traced into his brain,
And one of the multitudes only drove over the fountains,
Which he could dwell with, in solitude, never again.

# DREAMS SHALL COME TRUE

## I

Out of dim nothingness arose a song,
And it was wrapped in its own mystery.
No soul can tell from whence it rose to mind,
No more than he can tell whereto he goes;
I mean the true self, not the flesh and bone,
That are corruptible in their own way,
As thoughts in their way may be waste or fruitful.
Truths more commendable appear in music
Than in plain words, that match not with their beauty.
Far more the delicate tracery of ideas,
That no mere prose can bring into the mind,
Arises with the sound of moving words
That pass in unison athwart the ear.
For there are thoughts that no description lends
A visible appearance to, that lie
Like wild gazelles, or fleet to fastnesses
Where none may track them. But to the still mind
They wend with music in fair apparitions,
Which those who reverence them can make their own,
And in their heavenly qualities partake.
So to that heaven move the souls of those
Who came from heaven, and who visit there
While bound upon the wheel of life on earth.
Wherefrom the songs arise, that solace them,
The songs that never touch the mundane mind,
And which the wheel can never bind to earth.

## II

The heavenly visitants can never die,
And are not bound by aught of time or place,
But thoughts can be corrupted and debased
Even in the mind they meet in, for there darkle
The other visitants that not from heaven

Have traced their sources, that too never perish,
But are eternally at war with those
Who bring us beauty. Can the soul be master
Of those opposing forces, which with weapons
Flesh cannot war with, drive us to our places?
Which so defile the heavenly springs of being,
That though we are athirst, we will not drink?
The flesh also is with them like a giant,
And with its gross strength hales us from our havens;
And our own selves are traitors to our purpose,
And careless or despairing drive us downward,
Even to the holds that angels cannot visit;
And Time and Space so fetter us, that pinions
Which triumphed o'er them, now lie shorn and broken.

### III

Whoso would win to heaven courts no evil,
Or evil at the last shall bear him down,
But many things there are, that are not evil,
But evil shadows dwell within their structures.
If we allow them, like the horse of Troy,
Within our outworks, these will bring us ruin.
Must we, then, bar our city to all traffic,
And fear the Greeks that bring us earthly gifts?
Thus to the tomb we bear the solitude
We have in life created — is this good?

### IV

Man of the mind who listens to these numbers,
And cons in them the studious lore of ages,
Think, that from Good and Evil any presence
Can be created. In the minds of many
They rule like sceptred kings, and neither conquer
Nor yet are conquered. Whereto goes that mind?
Not into heaven, surely, with its devils,
Nor to the evil regions, where its angels

Can never bide. No, in far dissolution
At last that mind is driven, and its ashes
Are scattered by the winds to nothingness.

V

Let us at last see that no single maestro
Can sway for us the instruments of being,
Save that we have elected him to rule us.
What we prefer, we are, have been, and ever shall be.
If we would choose destruction, we shall have it,
And would we dwell in torment, we must bear it
As best we may, but neither any suffrance,
Nor our election, can from black destruction
Build up the mansions of a heavenly dwelling.

# MUSIC OF THE HEART

I play the organ of the human heart,
And it has pipes more than the mighty art
Of the musician ever can encompass.
The trumpets of its triumph peal their paean
To the far snowy summits of achievement.
Its viols of despair have for their meaning
The ruin of a universe, that gathers
In that concentered focus of a soul.
The laughter of the Earth's light-hearted children
Rings in those hollow cells, that know no sorrow,
And charm the happy hours from the tower
Wherein the hoar frost of the centuries
Has prisoned them, to live and pass in sunshine.
Its flutes can wake the sleeping minds of maidens,
And tell the youths of their mild mysteries,
Which no one yet has fathomed with his mind,
But which all men have measured with their hearts.
Such are the choral voices of our being,
That make our thoughts to be winged orisons,
Even to the nave of that serene cathedral
Which rests its roof upon the far horizon.

# THE TALE OF HADJI

Breathes there a man of my inconstant mind?
   I have not found that man or minister,
   Who, when the first frail fancies stir,
Is to impenetrable gloom consigned.

When there is fire within the hearts of age,
    Cold reason may delicious fonts immure.
   When the unstable minds of youth endure,
The heart may answer eloquence of sage.

I cannot wear the pearls of pure desire,
   With my first love defiled, her brain debased.
   Oh, all the fairest tissues Heaven graced
Could not again provoke my heart to fire.

Heaven's fire came down in momentary rage,
   And  a scarred trunk its blackened length uprears.
   Ye gentlefolk, stop if you will your ears,
While I relate of love another wage.

The young folk came, attracted by the blaze,
   And two conceived an idea in each brain,
   They too would draw Heaven's fire, and muchen fain,
Resolved to live together all their days.

The peaceful sound their happy voices wore,
   The whitewashed walls yet echoed with amaze.
Though dearly loved the rapture of the days,
Night's silent bliss succeeded o'er and o'er.

Upon the Monday morn they strongly strove,
   And Sunday was their last, their peaceful day.
   Delight to lie at gaze, the lady lay,
And watched the flamelets in the kitchen stove.

The sun risen higher on surcease of toil
  Shone on the barn and cowlot with strong ray,
  And on the mustard flower's yellow play,
Grown into splendor from the garden soil.

The careless shine awakened her small boy:
  With lusty lungs the yelling infant lay.
  The kicks and squirmings of his legs at play
Would be beyond the juggler's best employ.

"Servig'rous buzzard," 'gan she thus to say.
  "Oh, precious baby of my husband dear!"
  And as she gazed, a slowly rolling tear
Fell on the breast where reckless infant lay.

Indeed, he recked not of the heaven or earth,
  He only knew that hunger was his bane,
  And in sophisticated wise he twain
Did dry up ere he had exhausted worth.

And in a fellow feeling for the earth
  The husband wandered to the cowlot gate,
  To feed the cattle, who were wont, so late,
To lick their brindled backs, and moo for hay.

"Now, Sammy, what on airth," the grandam said,
  Beginning as he came into the house,
  As is the way of women, "ails the cows?"
"I don't know, mother, guess they oughta fed."

His wife still sat, with snowy ankles bare,
  The baby's tumbled clothes about her spread.
  "I don't know why you took him out of bed,"
He argued loudly, with a prideful air.

"He k'ies," said mother, "p'ecious itty fing,"
  And kissed his baby-blue, unwitting eyes,
  And after that she opened with surprise
*Her* blue ones, for her husband kissed her ring.

109

And a transfigured spirit sat upon
    The peaceful precincts of that household small.
    I know not who, but he is all in all,
And all his loving light I have foregone,

Save in half-lucid moments when the bliss
    That young folk wed for, beckons heart and head,
    Or memories again awake the dread,
Fierce spirit flaming from a lover's kiss.

Sweet story! Will ye take it for its worth,
    Ye gentlefolk, who erstwhile hung the head?
    It is no summons dutiful and dread,
No fire of wrath consuming half the earth.

But in another song the birds shall sing,
    The sweetbrier twine around the mouldered tree,
    While lily buds shall crop out on the lea,
And heather bells shall flower on the ling.

# THINGS THAT ARE

Gaily the glory gilds the wave
Along the path that the moonbeams pave.
Glory is gliding from star to star,
Gilding the beauty of things that are.
All things that are shall melt and mar;
   Music on farther sandy bar
Breaks and swells, but each moment tells
   Only the music that came before.
Where are the bells that music swells
   To songs that we never heard before?

Ever the voice of the turtle dove
Whispers the music of earthly love.
Season on season that mellow lore
Rises in beauty it never wore,
Breathes in softness o'er misty glen,
And gleams again on the lives of men.
   Sunlight loops, when the lily droops,
   Galaxies blue, and the starlight stoops,
And rises on wings that are lighter than air
   Over the stillness that gardens wear.

But melt and mar shall things that are,
   And is there never a fixed star?
Threes and sevens that gild the heavens
   Nightly sink, but to rise afar.
Stars are fixed, and the lives of men
Rolling return to the light again.
Gilds the glory each morning's gleam,
And silently glides the starry stream,
Building afar, o'er things that are,
Things that shall never pale nor mar.